Hard-to-Solve
Brainteasers

Official
American Mensa
puzzle book

Jaime & Lea Poniachik

Sterling Publishing Co., Inc.
New York

English version edited by Peter Gordon.

Translated from Spanish by Natalia M. Tizón.

Library of Congress Cataloging-in-Publication Data Available

10 9 8 7 6 5

Published by Sterling Publishing Company, Inc.
387 Park Avenue South, New York, N.Y. 10016
Originally published in Argentina and Spain by
Juegos & Co., S.R.L. and Zugarto Ediciones
under the title *Cómo Jugar y Divertirse con su Inteligencia*
© 1978 and 1996 by Jaime and Lea Poniachik
English translation © 1998 by Sterling Publishing Co., Inc.
Distributed in Canada by Sterling Publishing
% Canadian Manda Group, One Atlantic Avenue, Suite 105
Toronto, Ontario, Canada M6K 3E7
Distributed in Great Britain and Europe by Cassell PLC
Wellington House, 125 Strand, London WC2R 0BB, England
Distributed in Australia by Capricorn Link (Australia) Pty Ltd.
P.O. Box 6651, Baulkham Hills, Business Centre, NSW 2153, Australia

Sterling ISBN 0-8069-6153-8

Contents

Introduction
5

Puzzles
6

Hints
59

Answers
65

Index
92

Introduction

These brainteasers have two purposes: to let you have fun and to train your mind.

You don't need any special knowledge to solve them. It's a matter of thinking a little about the questions and applying common sense.

The puzzles are organized by order of difficulty. If you cannot find the answer to a problem and feel like giving up, refer to the "Hints" section for some clues in finding the answer.

Solving brainteasers can be a good activity for a solo player or a group, and can be turned into a game of competition.

1. Twins

Peter and Paul are twin brothers. One of them (we don't know which) always lies. The other one always tells the truth. I ask one of them:
"Is Paul the one that lies?"
"Yes," he answers.
Did I speak to Peter or Paul?

2. Twin Statistics

Suppose that 3% of births give rise to twins. What percentage of the population is a twin: 3%, less than 3%, or more than 3%?

3. Place Your Cards

You have three cards: an ace, a queen, and a six. One is a diamond, one is a heart, and one is a spade, although not necessarily in that order.
The diamond sits between the queen and the heart.
The six is immediately to the right of the spade.
Write in the picture below where each card is located.

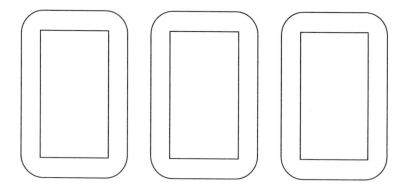

4. The Professor and His Friend

Professor Zizoloziz puts 40 matches on the table and explains a game to his friend Kathy.

Each player in turn takes 1, 3, or 5 matches. The winner is the one who takes the last match. Kathy chooses to go first and takes 3 matches.

Who do you think will win this game, Kathy or the professor?

5. Irregular Circuit

Two cars start from point A at the same time and drive around a circuit more than one mile in length. While they are driving laps around the circuit, each car must maintain a steady speed. Since one car is faster than the other, one car will pass the other at certain points. The first pass occurs 150 yards from point A.

At what distance from A will one car pass the other again?

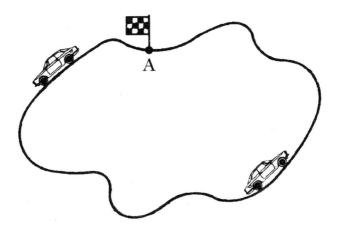

6. Economical Progression

Below are four terms in an arithmetic progression (a series in which the difference between terms is constant, in this case 50):

5, 55, 105, 155

Notice how the four terms use only three different digits: 0, 1, and 5.

Can you find six terms in an arithmetic progression that use only three different digits?

7. Skin and Shoes

A white man is wearing a pair of white shoes, a black man is wearing a pair of black shoes, and a red-skinned man is wearing a pair of red shoes. In a gesture of friendship, they decide to exchange shoes. When they are done, each man has on one shoe from each of the other two men.

How many shoes will you have to look at to know which color of shoe each man is wearing on each foot; that is, which color shoe each man wears on his right foot and which color each man wears on his left foot? Note that when you look at a shoe, you can see that man's skin color.

8. Up and Down

This morning I had to take the stairs because the elevator was out of service. I had already gone down seven steps when I saw Professor Zizoloziz on the ground floor coming up. I continued descending at my usual pace, greeted the professor when we passed, and was surprised to see that when I still had four more steps to go, the professor had gone up the whole flight. "When I go down one step, he goes up two," I thought.

How many steps does the staircase have?

Hard-to-Solve Brainteasers

9. What Month—I

A month begins on a Friday and ends on a Friday, too. What month is it?

10. What Month—II

The result of adding the date of the last Monday of last month and the date of the first Thursday of next month is 38. If both dates are of the same year, what is the current month?

11. Eve's Enigma

After heaven, the earth, the grass, and all the animals were created, the snake, who was very smart, decided to make its own contribution.

It decided to lie every Tuesday, Thursday and Saturday. For the other days of the week, it told the truth.

"Eve, dear Eve, why don't you try an apple?" the snake suggested.

"But I am not allowed to!" said Eve.

"Oh, no!" said the snake. "You can eat it today since it is Saturday and God is resting."

"No, not today," said Eve, "Maybe tomorrow."

"Tomorrow is Wednesday and it will be too late," insisted the snake.

This is how the snake tricked Eve.

What day of the week did this conversation take place?

12. Broken M

We have formed six triangles by drawing three straight lines on the M. That's not enough. Starting with a new M, form nine triangles by drawing three straight lines.

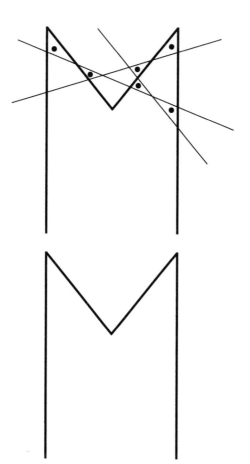

13. Soccer Scores—I

A soccer tournament has just ended. Five teams participated and each one played once against each of the other teams. The winner of a match received 2 points, the losing team 0 points, and each team received 1 point for a tie.

The final results were:

Lions	6 points
Tigers	5 points
Bears	3 points
Orioles	1 point

We are missing one team, the Eagles. What was their point total?

14. Soccer Scores—II

In a three-team tournament, each team played once against each of the two other teams. Each team scored one goal.

The final results were:

Lions	3 points
Tigers	2 points
Bears	1 point

What was the score in each match?

15. What Time Is It—I

I'm looking at my watch. From this moment on, the hour hand will take exactly twice as long as the minute hand to reach the number six. What time is it?

16. What Time Is It—II

I'm looking at my watch. From this moment on, the hour hand will take exactly three times longer than the minute hand to reach the number six. What time is it?

17. What Time Is It—III

I'm looking at my watch. The hour hand is on one mark and the minute hand is on the next one. (By marks, we mean minute marks.) What time is it?

18. What Time Is It—IV

I'm looking at my watch. The hour hand is on one mark and the minute hand is on the previous one. (By marks, we mean minute marks.) What time is it?

19. Prohibited Connection

Using numbers 1, 2, 3, 4, 5, and 6, put each of them in a circle. There is only one condition. The circles connected by a line cannot have consecutive numbers. For example, 4 cannot be connected with 3 or 5.

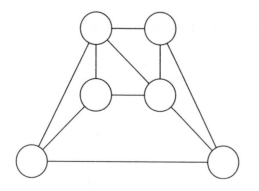

20. Concentric

The big square has an area of 60 square inches. Is there a fast way to figure out what the area of the small square is?

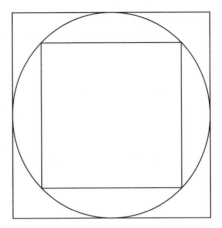

21. John Cash

John Cash saw his face on a poster nailed to a tree. As he approached, he saw "WANTED, DEAD OR ALIVE." Under his picture, it read "REWARD: ___ DOLLARS."

There was a three-digit figure on the poster. John drew his Colt and shot at the first number (in the hundreds column).

He had just reduced the price on his head by five times.

"Good Lord!" said the doctor's daughter, who was sitting on the other side of the tree doing her math homework.

John blushed, and shot again at another number (in the tens column).

He had just reduced the price on his head by another five times.

"Nice shooting!" said the young girl.

"Thank you, miss," said John. He spurred his horse and never returned.

What was the initial reward offered on John's head?

22. Russian Roulette

Russian roulette was created by Count Ugo Lombardo Fiumiccino, who successfully died during his first presentation of it.

He placed six jars on a shelf, as in the drawing below. After staring at them, he closed his eyes and told his friend to fill them up with the ingredients, making sure that each jar contained an ingredient other than the one shown on its label.

When she was finished, the count asked:

"Dear Petrushka, would you be so kind as to tell me where the salt is?"

"Under the jar containing snuff," answered Petrushka.

"My dear friend, would you tell me where the sugar is?" he asked.

"Immediately to the right of the jar containing coffee," she answered.

Ugo Lombardo Fiumiccino, confirming his desire to commit suicide, reached immediately for the jar containing arsenic.

Where is the arsenic?

Hard-to-Solve Brainteasers

23. New Race

Two cars start traveling from two different points and in opposite directions in a circuit race at a constant speed. The cars cross for the first time at point A. The second time is at point B. The third time is at point C, and the fourth one is again at point A.

How much faster is one car going than the other?

24. The Calculator Keys

Several times Professor Zizoloziz mentioned that he feels uncomfortable looking at his pocket calculator. Yesterday, he was elated because he had found the reason why. The layout of the keys from 1 to 9 and the "minus" and "equal" signs look like they are doing subtraction. It's an incorrect one however, because 789 minus 456 does not equal 123. Zizoloziz thought of changing the numbers to achieve a correct equation. He changed 7 with 3, then 3 with 4, and 9 with 6, resulting in 486 – 359 = 127. He made only three changes to achieve this.

Using the keypad below as a reference, can you obtain a correctly subtracted number with only two changes?

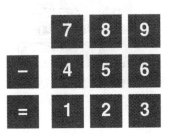

25. Nice Discounts

A bookstore has a nice discount policy. If you buy a $20 book today, you get a 2% discount on your next purchase. If you buy a $15 book, you get a 1.5% discount on your next purchase. If you have to buy three books that cost $10, $20, and $30, you could buy the $30 book today, the $10 tomorrow (on which you'll get a 3% discount), and the $20 book the following day (on which you'll get a 1% discount). Or you could buy the $30 book and the $20 book today, and the $10 book tomorrow (with a 5% discount).

What is the cheapest way to buy five books priced at $10, $20, $30, $40, and $50?

26. Enigmatic Fares

Professor Zizoloziz always adds the five digits on a bus transfer. Yesterday, he rode route 62 with a friend. As soon as he got the tickets, which were consecutively numbered, he added the numbers on them and then told his friend that the sum of all ten digits was exactly 62. His logical friend asked him if the sum of the numbers on either of the tickets was by any chance 35. Professor Zizoloziz answered and his friend then knew the numbers on the bus tickets.

What were the numbers on the two bus tickets?

27. Horoscope

An indiscreet young man asks his beautiful mathematics teacher her age. She responds, "Today's date is my age, although before this week is over there will be another day with a date one fifth of the new age that I will be."

What is the teacher's sign of the zodiac?

28. Strangers in the Night

The midnight train is coming down the Strujen-Bajen mountains. Art Farnanski seems to be dozing off in his seat.

Someone knows that this is not true.

At the station, all the passengers get off the train, except one. The conductor comes and taps him on the shoulder to let him know they have arrived. Art Farnanski does not answer. He is dead.

"His heart?" asks commander Abrojos, looking at the dead body.

"Strychnine," answers the forensic doctor.

Hours later, the four people that had shared the train compartment with the dead man are at the police station.

The man in the dark suit:
"I'm innocent. The blonde woman was talking to Farnanski."

The blonde woman:
"I'm innocent. I did not speak to Farnanski."

The man in the light suit:
"I'm innocent. The brunette woman killed him."

The brunette woman:
"I'm innocent. One of the men killed him."

That same morning, while he is serving him coffee, the waiter at the Petit Piccolo asks commander Abrojos:

"This is an easy case for you, isn't it?"

"Yes," answers the commander. "Four true statements and four false ones. Easy as pie."

Who killed Farnanski? (Only one person is guilty.)

29. Monte Carlo

The famous playboy Hystrix Tardigradus explained to a beautiful woman his system for playing roulette:

"In each round, I always bet half of the money I have at the time on red. Yesterday, I counted and I had won as many rounds as I had lost."

Over the course of the night, did Hystrix win, lose, or break even?

30. The Foreigners and the Menu

A particular inn always offers the same nine dishes on its dinner menu: A, B, C, D, E, F, G, H, and I.

Five foreigners arrive. Nobody tells them which dish corresponds to each letter and so they each select one letter without knowing what they will eat.

The innkeeper arrives with the five dishes ordered and puts them in the center of the table so that they can decide who eats what.

This goes on for two more nights.

The foreigners, who are professors of logic, were able to deduce by the dishes they ordered which letter represents what dish.

What could have been the dishes ordered each of the three nights?

31. Fort Knox Jumping Frogs—I

The first puzzle of this series is very well known. We included it here, though, because it is good practice for the following puzzles, since they all use the same method of moving coins.

Make a line of eight coins. In four moves, make four piles of two coins each.

A move consists of taking one coin, skipping over two others, and piling it on top of the next one.

The answers list one of several possible solutions for all of the puzzles in this series.

32. Fort Knox Jumping Frogs—II

Place 14 coins in the shape of a cross, as shown in the illustration. In seven moves as described in the Puzzle 31, make seven piles of two coins each. Note: Only move the coins in a straight line; do not change directions.

33. Fort Knox Jumping Frogs—III

Place 12 coins on the three rings as shown in the illustration below. In six moves as described in the Puzzle 31, make six piles of two coins each. Note: Only move the coins around their own rings and always go clockwise in direction.

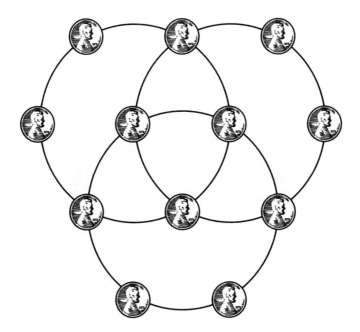

34. Fort Knox Jumping Frogs—IV

Place 20 coins in the shape of a star as shown in the illustration below. In ten moves as described in the Puzzle 31, make ten piles of two coins each. Note: Only move the coins along the straight lines and do not turn corners.

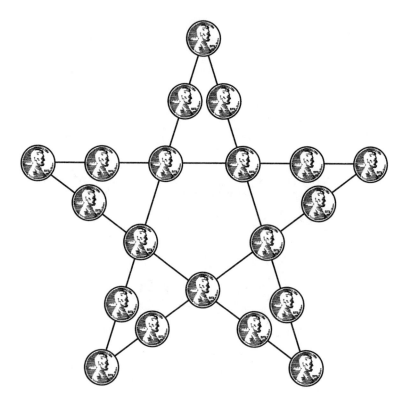

Hard-to-Solve Brainteasers

35. Fort Knox Jumping Frogs—V

Place 20 coins in a four-by-five rectangle as shown below. In ten moves as described in the Puzzle 31, make ten piles of two coins each. Note: Coins can move only in a straight line and cannot move diagonally.

36. The Harem

The story goes that the harem of the Great Tamerlan was protected by a door with many locks. A vizier and four slaves were in charge of guarding this door.

Knowledgeable of the weaknesses of men, the Great Tamerlan had distributed the keys in such a way that the vizier could only open the door if he was with any one of the slaves, and the slaves could only open it if three of them worked together.

How many locks did the door have?

37. The Dividing End

My ID number is quite remarkable. It's a nine-digit number with each of the digits from 1 to 9 appearing once. The whole number is divisible by 9. If you remove the rightmost digit, the remaining eight-digit number is divisible by 8. Removing the next rightmost digit leaves a seven-digit number that is divisible by 7. This property continues all the way down to one digit. What is my ID number?

38. The Island and the Englishmen

On a deserted island (except for a small group of Englishmen) there are four clubs.

The membership lists reveal that:

a) Each Englishman is a member of two clubs.

b) Every set of two clubs has only one member in common.

How many Englishmen are there on the island?

39. Logic Apples

Four perfect logicians, who all knew each other from being members of the Perfect Logicians' Club, sat around a table that had a dish with 11 apples in it. The chat was intense, and they ended up eating all the apples. Everybody had at least one apple, and everyone knew that fact, and each logician knew the number of apples that he ate. They didn't know how many apples each of the others ate, though. They agreed to ask only questions that they didn't know the answers to:

Alonso: Did you eat more apples than I did, Bertrand?

Bertrand: I don't know. Did you, George, eat more apples than I did?

George: I don't know.

Kurt: Aha!

Kurt figured out how many apples each person ate. Can you do the same?

40. Added Corners

Using the numbers from 1 to 8, place one in each shape with one condition: The number in each square has to be the sum of its two neighboring circles.

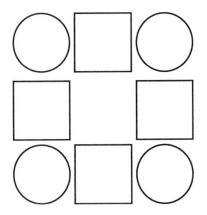

41. Rectangles

The vertical rectangle (solid line) has an area of 40 square inches.

Find out in a quick way the area of the inclined rectangle (dotted line).

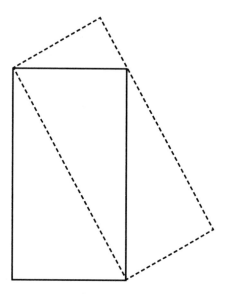

42. A Warm Farewell

At a train station, the Porter family is saying good-bye to the Robinson family. We don't know who is leaving and who is staying.

Each of the members of the Porter family says farewell to each of the members of the Robinson family. To say good-bye, two men shake hands, and both a man and a woman and two women kiss once on the cheek.

An eyewitness to the event counted 21 handshakes and 34 kisses.

How many men and how many women were saying good-bye?

43. Four Minus One Is a Crime

Messrs. A, B, C, and D met last night in a corner in the cir-
cled area. After the meeting, each of them went home,
except for one, Mr. D, who was discovered dead this morning in the river.

"Did you take the statements from the three suspects?"

"Yes, commissioner. Mr. A declared that from the corner
of the meeting he walked 7 blocks to get home. Mr. B said
that he walked 6 blocks to get home. Mr. C answered that
he walked 5 blocks to get home. I marked their homes on
the map."

"And in which corner did they meet?"

"Nobody remembers."

"Do you want to know something? It isn't necessary,
because I know that one of the three suspects is lying."

"And that is the killer!"

"Brilliant deduction!"

Who is the killer?

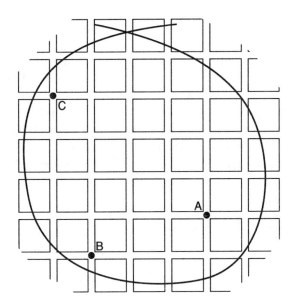

44. On the Route of Marco Polo

On his way east, Marco Polo passed five little villages along a straight road. At each village a road sign points to one of the other four villages. Below are the five signs, in no particular order. Can you add the corresponding arrows to the four signs that have lost them? (The five signs are all on the same side of the road.)

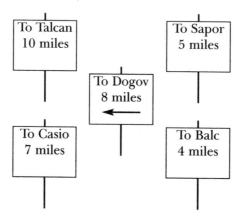

45. On the Road

On my way to Philadelphia, I pass five mileposts that indicate their respective distances to Philadelphia. The mileposts are at fixed intervals. What's curious is that each milepost has a two-digit number, and together the five mileposts use all the digits from 0 to 9 once. What is the smallest distance that the closest milepost can be from Philadelphia? (As usual, mileposts don't begin with 0.)

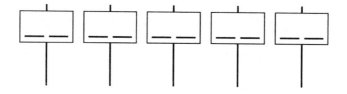

46. Touching Squares

Shown here are three squares on a table with each one touching the other two squares. If you want to place squares so that each square touches exactly three other squares (not counting corner-to-corner or corner-to-side contact), how many squares do you need? All squares must lie on the table surface.

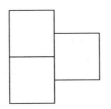

47. Equal Vision

Each watchman looks in all directions (horizontal, vertical, and diagonal). On the left board, each watchman has five vacant cells under his gaze. (A watchman can see beyond another watchman.) On the right, each watchman can see six empty cells. What's the maximum number of watchmen that can be placed so that each sees seven empty cells?

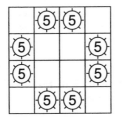 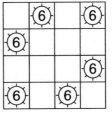

48. Blood and Sand

"You are the killer!" declared Commissioner Abrojos. His assistant, Inspector Begonias, slanted his eyes and looked around. They were alone in the room.

"I don't understand," he said.

"You are the killer!" the commissioner repeated.

Here is the story:

Yesterday, responding to a phone call, Inspector Begonias visited the mansion of millionaire Lincoln Dustin at around 7 P.M. The millionaire was dead in his office. There were blood stains on the carpet around the desk. Begonias inspected the place. He questioned the butler, who told him that Lincoln Dustin always led a perfectly ordered life. Every day, at noon, Mr. Dustin started the hourglass, the one that was now next to his dead body. At exactly midnight, the hourglass finished and Lincoln Dustin would go to sleep.

Begonias thought this was all very interesting, but not so useful for his investigation. That same night, the butler's call woke him up.

"Inspector!" cried the butler, "The hourglass did not finish at midnight, but at 3 A.M.!"

Begonias told all of this to Commissioner Abrojos.

"Let's suppose," said the commissioner, "that Mr. Dustin was able to turn the hourglass to leave us a clue as to the time of the crime."

Begonias nodded.

"In that case," continued the commissioner, "you told me that you had gone to the mansion around 7 P.M., which makes me think that you are the killer."

This is how they reached the conversation at the beginning of our puzzle.

Begonias could not believe it.

"I never thought," he said sadly, "that you would do this to me."

"Come on, Begonias, aren't you going to try to find an excuse?"

The inspector thought for a moment, going over the events of the previous day.

"The hourglass!" he cried. "I remember now. When I inspected the room I saw that the hourglass was on a hand-written note."

"Do you mean that the victim wrote the name of the killer? I don't believe that."

"Not at all!" said Begonias. "I wanted to read the note, so I lifted the hourglass and then I must have turned it upside down by mistake."

"What time was it then?"

"7 P.M."

"My dear friend, this clears you as a suspect!" said the commissioner.

Suppose that Mr. Dustin was able to invert the hourglass before dying. At what time did he die? Why did the commissioner consider Begonias as a suspect?

49. International Summit

At a recent international summit, five delegates (A, B, C, D, and E) participated. This is what we observed:

1. B and C spoke English, although when D joined them, they all changed to Spanish, the only common language among the three of them.

2. The only common language among A, B, and E was French.

3. The only common language between C and E was Italian.

4. Three delegates could speak Portuguese.

5. The most common language was Spanish.

6. One of the delegates spoke all five languages, another one spoke four, one spoke three, one spoke two, and the other only spoke one language.

What languages did each delegate speak?

50. Mister Digit Face

Place each of the digits 1 to 9, one digit per blank, so that the product of the two eyes equals the number above the head, and the product of each eye and mouth equals the number on the respective side of the face.

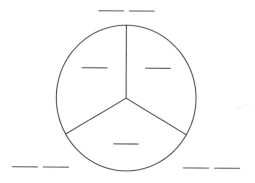

51. Digit Tree

Using each digit from 1 to 9 once, make seven numbers so that each number is equal to the sum of the numbers in the circles that are connected to it from below. (The numbers can be more than one digit.) There are two slightly different answers.

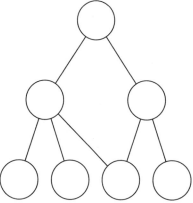

Hard-to-Solve Brainteasers

52. Figures to Cut in Two

Each one of the following figures can be divided into two equal parts (that may be mirror images of each other). The dividing lines can follow the grid or not. The grid is only to provide proportion to the figures.

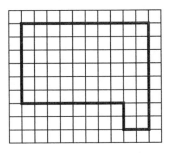
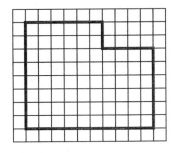

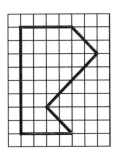
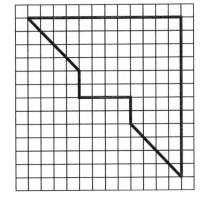

53. Segments

Place the digits 1 to 9 (using each digit once, one digit per box) so that:
- the boxes containing the 1 and 2 and all the ones between them add up to 12,
- the boxes containing the 2 and 3 and all the ones between them add up to 23,
- the boxes containing the 3 and 4 and all the ones between them add up to 34,
- the boxes containing the 4 and 5 and all the ones between them add up to 45.

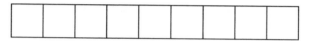

54. Multiple Towers

As the elevator rises along the eight-floor tower, it forms a series of three-digit numbers by combining the 72 in the elevator with the digit on the floor. What's more, these three-digit numbers are multiples of 2, 3, 4, etc., up to 9. (That is, on the lowest floor, 726 is evenly divisible by 2, on the next floor, 723 is evenly divisible by 3, and so on.) Can you find another arrangement for the digits 0 to 9 (using each digit once, one digit per box) so that the elevator isn't 72 and the combinations of the elevator with the level form an appropriate multiple?

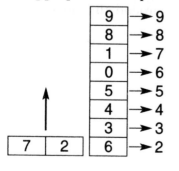

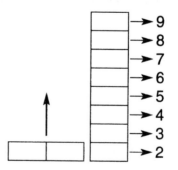

Hard-to-Solve Brainteasers

55. Earthlings

August 2002.

The spaceship landed.

"Earth!" they shouted.

They knew that earthlings are divided into three groups: those who always tell the truth, those who always lie, and those who do both, alternating between true and false statements, starting with either.

"Let's go!" said the captain.

The aliens approached three earthlings, who each were from a different group, and asked, "Who won the last World Cup? Who came in second? Who came in third?"

One of them responded, "Zaire first. Uruguay second. Spain third."

Another one said, "Zaire first. Spain second. Uruguay third."

The third one said, "Uruguay first. Spain second. Zaire third."

The aliens returned to their spaceship and flew back to where they came from.

Do you know which response was the true ranking in the World Cup?

56. The Ant and the Clock

Precisely when the big hand of the clock passes 12, an ant begins crawling counterclockwise around the clock from the 6 mark at a consistent speed.

When reaching the big hand of the clock, the ant turns around and, at the same speed, starts marching around the clock in the opposite direction.

Exactly 45 minutes after the first meeting, the ant crosses the big hand for the second time and dies.

How long has the ant been walking?

57. Hidden Word—I

A four-letter word belongs in the rectangle below. You are given several clues to help guess what it is.

In the column marked "2," you have words that share exactly two letters in the same position as the hidden word. For example, if the hidden word were REDO, in column 2 we could put DEMO, BEDS, DODO, etc. Column 1 contains words that share exactly one letter in the same position as the hidden word. In the example above, REDO being the hidden word, column 1 could have NODS, ROAD, etc.

Column 0 has words that do not share any letter in the same position as the hidden word. For our example, column 0 could have GAME, HARD, etc.

Now find the hidden word.

0	1	2
CULT	SOME	VEST
	HINT	HOSE

58. Hidden Word—II

A three-letter word belongs in the rectangle below. Given the words below, figure out what it is.

```
┌─────────────────────┐
│                     │
└─────────────────────┘
  0        1        2
 HAS      CON      SON
          CAB
```

59. Hidden Word—III

A five-letter word belongs in the rectangle below. Given the words below, figure out what it is.

```
┌─────────────────────┐
│                     │
└─────────────────────┘
  0        1        2
 BALKS    MILES    MUSHY
 GUSTO    GAUDY    PATES
```

Secret Number

In the first field of the first row of every illustration we have written (in invisible ink) a number formed by four different digits between 0 and 9.

The following rows indicate attempts to find out the secret number. Each try has, in the column to the right, its grade with letters R (right) and B (bingo). Each R indicates that this number has one digit in common with the secret number, but in a different position. Each B indicates that the number has one digit in common with the secret number in the same position.

Find out the secret number in the following tables.

60. Secret Number—I

				B	B	B	B
8	9	5	1	R	R		
2	1	6	9	R	B		
3	6	9	4	R	B		
4	7	2	1	R	B		
1	2	3	7	R	R	R	

61. Secret Number—II

				B	B	B	B
6	2	5	3	R			
8	1	4	7	R	R		
2	5	7	1	B			
3	6	0	9	R	R		
9	6	8	7	B	B		

62. Secret Number—III

				B	B	B	B
1	0	2	9	R			
3	4	6	2	R	R		
5	8	4	9	R	R		
8	5	2	1	R	R		
4	2	8	5	R	R	R	

63. Secret Number—IV

				B	B	B	B
3	9	2	0	R	R	R	
8	7	4	5	B			
9	0	7	5	R	R		
8	3	9	7	R	R	R	

64. Secret Number—V

				B	B	B	B
1	2	5	9	R			
1	3	8	9	R	B		
1	3	5	7	B	B		
4	3	9	7	B	B		

Hard-to-Solve Brainteasers

Dominoes

Each one of the following diagrams uses the 28 dominoes of a domino set to make a table. The values of each domino are written down in numbers instead of in dots, but we have not identified the individual dominoes. That's exactly what you'll have to do. In the first tables, we have helped you with some of them.

Notice that each table contains the 28 dominoes and no tile appears twice in the same table. Below each table you will find a list of the 28 dominoes so that you can track what you have found and what you are still missing.

(Dominoes was created by Mr. Lech Pijanovsky, from Poland.)

65. Table I

Find the 28 dominoes.

1	5	5	3	0	6	0	6
5	4	4	2	4	4	6	2
2	6	0	1	1	2	5	1
4	3	5	5	3	2	6	0
0	3	0	3	3	3	1	0
5	2	6	2	3	6	0	1
4	5	6	4	1	4	2	1

Here is a list of the 28 dominoes:

0-0						
0-1	1-1					
0-2	1-2	2-2				
0-3	1-3	2-3	3-3			
0-4	1-4	2-4	3-4	4-4		
0-5	1-5	2-5	3-5	4-5	5-5	
0-6	1-6	2-6	3-6	4-6	5-6	6-6

66. Table II

Find the 28 dominoes.

3	1	2	2	6	1	3	4
5	5	3	4	0	5	3	2
2	6	5	1	1	2	0	0
1	1	0	6	0	3	3	0
0	6	4	3	6	5	4	5
3	2	5	4	0	1	6	2
5	4	6	4	2	4	6	1

Here is a list of the 28 dominoes:
```
0-0
0-1  1-1
0-2  1-2  2-2
0-3  1-3  2-3  3-3
0-4  1-4  2-4  3-4  4-4
0-5  1-5  2-5  3-5  4-5  5-5
0-6  1-6  2-6  3-6  4-6  5-6  6-6
```

67. Table III

Find the 28 dominoes.

1	0	2	2	3	6	5
1	6	6	4	3	6	5
2	3	5	0	1	4	6
0	4	3	0	2	4	0
3	6	5	4	5	4	1
0	0	5	1	3	1	2
3	6	2	2	5	3	2
1	1	4	0	4	6	5

Here is a list of the 28 dominoes:

0-0						
0-1	1-1					
0-2	1-2	2-2				
0-3	1-3	2-3	3-3			
0-4	1-4	2-4	3-4	4-4		
0-5	1-5	2-5	3-5	4-5	5-5	
0-6	1-6	2-6	3-6	4-6	5-6	6-6

68. Table IV

Find the 28 dominoes.

5	4	2	3	6	3	4
4	6	5	5	0	6	3
4	6	2	3	4	1	2
6	0	6	3	0	4	1
0	6	0	2	3	4	2
5	5	6	1	4	5	3
5	1	3	2	2	1	1
1	5	2	0	1	0	0

Here is a list of the 28 dominoes:
0-0
0-1 1-1
0-2 1-2 2-2
0-3 1-3 2-3 3-3
0-4 1-4 2-4 3-4 4-4
0-5 1-5 2-5 3-5 4-5 5-5
0-6 1-6 2-6 3-6 4-6 5-6 6-6

69. Table V

Find the 28 dominoes.

4	0	0	1	1	1	0
5	2	3	5	6	5	6
3	5	4	4	3	4	2
2	0	0	5	6	5	3
2	2	1	5	6	0	1
2	4	4	3	2	6	4
5	6	0	3	2	3	6
1	1	3	6	4	1	0

Here is a list of the 28 dominoes:
0-0
0-1 1-1
0-2 1-2 2-2
0-3 1-3 2-3 3-3
0-4 1-4 2-4 3-4 4-4
0-5 1-5 2-5 3-5 4-5 5-5
0-6 1-6 2-6 3-6 4-6 5-6 6-6

70. Table VI

Find the 28 dominoes.

4	5	1	6	0	5	1
2	5	3	5	3	6	5
6	2	0	4	2	2	6
6	6	2	0	5	3	3
3	1	1	2	3	6	4
4	0	3	1	0	0	4
4	1	2	1	4	5	3
5	1	2	0	0	4	6

Here is a list of the 28 dominoes:
0-0
0-1   1-1
0-2   1-2   2-2
0-3   1-3   2-3   3-3
0-4   1-4   2-4   3-4   4-4
0-5   1-5   2-5   3-5   4-5   5-5
0-6   1-6   2-6   3-6   4-6   5-6   6-6

71. Hound—I

A hound started on a square numbered 1, and moved from square to square numbering them in succession to the last one, numbered 20. The hound moved horizontally and vertically only, never entering any square twice. The numbers were then deleted. All we know is that the squares with circles had the numbers 5, 10, and 15, in some order. Figure out the path of the hound.

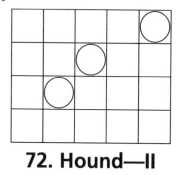

72. Hound—II

A hound started on a square numbered 1, and moved from square to square numbering them in succession to the last one, numbered 35. The hound moved horizontally and vertically only, never entering any square twice. The numbers were then deleted. All we know is that the squares with circles had the numbers 7, 14, 21, 28, and 35, in some order. Figure out the path of the hound.

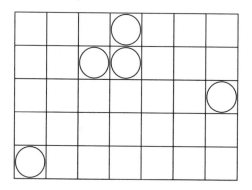

Hard-to-Solve Brainteasers

73. Hound—III

A hound started on a square numbered 1, and moved from square to square numbering them in succession to the last one, numbered 25. The hound never entered any square twice and moved horizontally and vertically only, except for one diagonal move to a neighboring square. All the numbers except those shown were then deleted. Figure out the path of the hound.

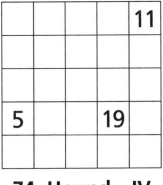

74. Hound—IV

A hound started on a square numbered 1, and moved from square to square numbering them in succession to the last one, numbered 25. The hound never entered any square twice and moved horizontally and vertically only, except for one jump move like a chess knight, shown below left. All the numbers except those shown were then deleted. Figure out the path of the hound.

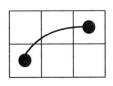

75. Hound—V

A hound started on a square numbered 1, and moved from square to square numbering them in succession to the last one, numbered 9. The hound never entered any square twice and moved horizontally and vertically only. The prime numbers in the grid formed a symmetric pattern. Figure out the path of the hound in the bigger board where the prime numbers (2, 3, 5, 7, 11, 13, 17, 19, and 23) form a symmetric pattern. One number has been supplied. There are two answers.

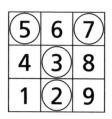

				6

Poker

We have a set of 28 poker cards (with 8, 9, 10, J, Q, K, and A). We select 25 and make a five-by-five table, like in the drawings.

We then have twelve "hands" of five cards (five horizontally, five vertically, and two diagonally). Next to each "hand" we write its combination.

Pair: two cards of the same value.

Two pair: two pairs plus a fifth card.

Three of a kind: three cards of equal value.

Full house: three of a kind with a pair.

Four of a kind: four cards of the same value.

Straight: five cards of consecutive values. The ace can be high or low, so the possible combinations of a straight are: A-8-9-10-J, 8-9-10-J-Q, 9-10-J-Q-K, and 10-J-Q-K-A.

Straight flush: a straight where all cards are of the same suit.

(We write "nothing" when we have none of these combinations.)

Important: The cards of each "hand" do not have to be in order. For example, the line containing the straight can have a 9, then an 8, then a J, then a 10, then an A.

Find the values (just the values, not the suits) of all cards left blank.

76. Poker—I

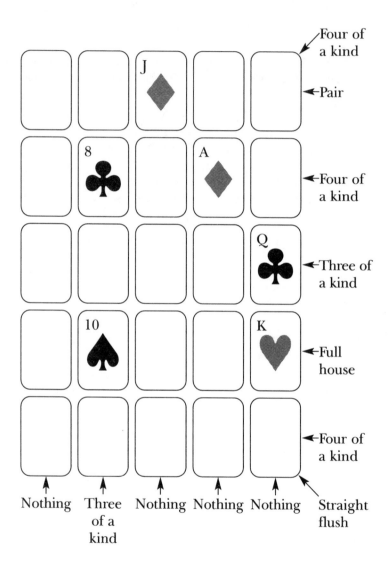

Find the values (just the values, not the suits) of all cards left blank.

Hard-to-Solve Brainteasers

77. Poker—II

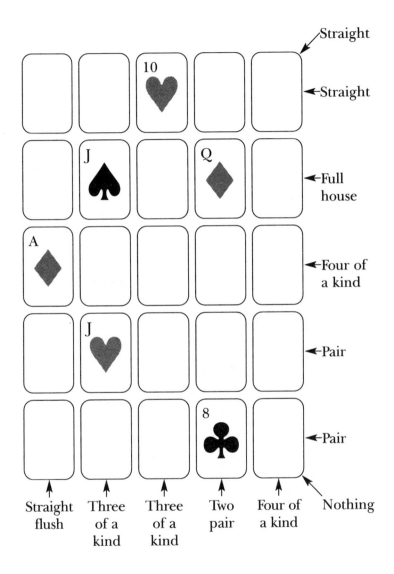

Find the values (just the values, not the suits) of all cards left blank.

78. Poker—III

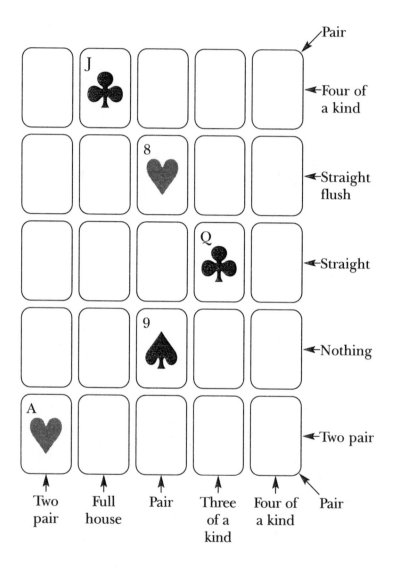

Find the values (just the values, not the suits) of all cards left blank.

Hard-to-Solve Brainteasers

79. Poker—IV

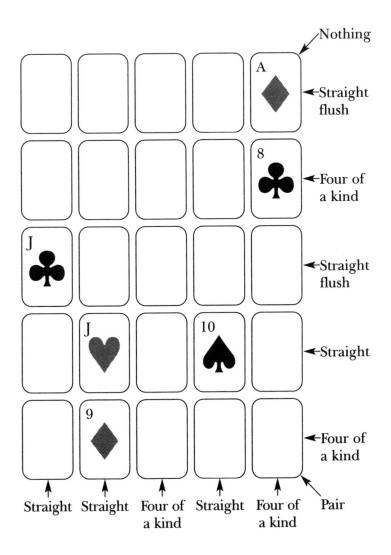

Find the values (just the values, not the suits) of all cards left blank.

80. Poker—V

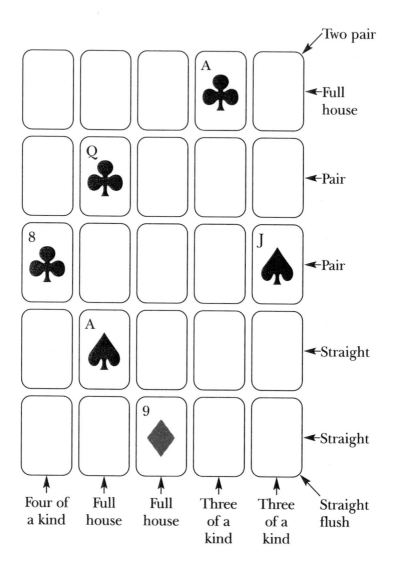

Find the values (just the values, not the suits) of all cards left blank.

Hard-to-Solve Brainteasers

81. Poker—VI

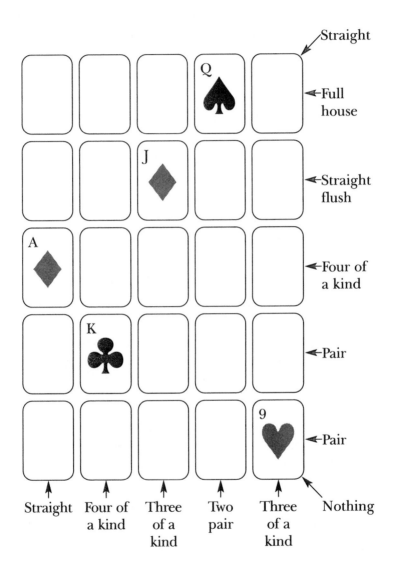

Find the values (just the values, not the suits) of all cards left blank.

Hints

Here are clues to help solve the problems.

1. TWINS. If a person always lies or always tells the truth, can he call himself a liar?

2. TWIN STATISTICS. Imagine there are 100 births, with 3% being twin births. How many people are born?

3. PLACE YOUR CARDS. Place the diamond by following the first clue given in the puzzle. You can now tell what the queen's suit is.

4. THE PROFESSOR AND HIS FRIEND. Did you notice that each player takes an odd number of matches?

5. IRREGULAR CIRCUIT. Why not take the first pass as a new starting point?

6. ECONOMICAL PROGRESSION. The three digits are 1, 2, and 6.

7. SKIN AND SHOES. Look at one foot and count the rest.

8. UP AND DOWN. The professor had an advantage of 11 steps and is climbing at twice my speed.

9. WHAT MONTH—I. It must be a strange month, right?

10. WHAT MONTH—II. Note that 38 is a very high number for the sum of the first Thursday of a month and of the last Monday of another month. What days could give such a high result?

11. EVE'S ENIGMA. The snake tells Eve that today is Saturday and tomorrow is Wednesday. Isn't that odd? On what days of the week can the snake talk like that?

12. BROKEN M. It might be useful to draw three straight lines on a white piece of paper and then draw an M on top of them.

13. SOCCER SCORES—I. How many games were played in the tournament? How many points in total were there in the entire tournament?

14. SOCCER SCORES—II. What were the scores for the games played by the Lions? What were the scores for the Bears?

15-18. WHAT TIME IS IT. Think of a time, say, 3 o'clock. Are the conditions of the problem true for the time you just thought of? In what area of the clock are we closer to the conditions of the puzzle?

19. PROHIBITED CONNECTION. Notice that the number 1 can be connected with five other digits. This does not occur for 2, 3, 4, or 5.

20. CONCENTRIC. Move the figure. What happens when you rotate the small square?

21. JOHN CASH. When John erased the first number, there was a two-digit number left. Think about it. If you remove the number in the tens column, this two-digit number is divided by five.

22. RUSSIAN ROULETTE. By the first answer you know that the snuff/salt pair is vertical. Can it be on the right side? Remember that a jar never contains the ingredient shown on the label.

23. NEW RACE. Take A as the starting point.

24. THE CALCULATOR KEYS. This puzzle has two solutions. Give it a try.

25. NICE DISCOUNTS. Buy all the books in just two days.

26. ENIGMATIC FARES. The tickets have consecutive numbers. The sum of the digits of both is 62, an even number. What is the last digit of the first ticket?

27. HOROSCOPE. Without doubt, this is a very special date.

28. STRANGERS IN THE NIGHT. There are exactly four true statements. Only one person is guilty. What does this mean about the "I'm innocent" statements?

29. MONTE CARLO. Let's say that you start with $100. If you lose and win, what happens to your money?

30. THE FOREIGNERS AND THE MENU. Out of the five dishes they order each night, could it be that two of them are the same?

31-35. FORT KNOX JUMPING FROGS. Play with some coins.

36. THE HAREM. Try it. If the door had 3 locks, could the Great Tamerlan's system work?

37. THE DIVIDING END. Let's call the ID number ABCDEFGHI. ABCDE can be divided evenly by 5, so we know what E is.

38. THE ISLAND AND THE ENGLISHMEN. Draw 4 circles that represent the clubs. Connect the clubs to the members.

39. LOGIC APPLES. Alonso would not have asked the question if he had eaten 5 or more apples, because nobody could have eaten more than him.

40. ADDED CORNERS. Place the 8 first. Can it be in a corner?

41. RECTANGLES. Find a simple way to divide the figure.

42. A WARM FAREWELL. Add the number of handshakes and kisses. It comes to a total of 55. If each Porter said good-bye to each Robinson, the number of the Porter family members multiplied by the number of the Robinson family members must equal 55.

43. FOUR MINUS ONE IS A CRIME. Go from A to B on the map. Try different routes. Count how many blocks you travel every time. Compare it with the suspects' statements.

44. ON THE ROUTE OF MARCO POLO. Each sign points to a different village. What can be said of the sum of the distances in each direction?

45. ON THE ROAD. From one sign to the next the tens' column must change.

46. TOUCHING SQUARES. You'll need more than 10 squares.

47. EQUAL VISION. It can be done with three or four watchmen. Can you do it with more?

48. BLOOD AND SAND. Why did the commissioner suspect Begonias? Put yourself in his shoes. You do not know that Begonias inverted the hourglass, but instead you believe that Lincoln Dustin did it when dying.

49. INTERNATIONAL SUMMIT. Use the table on the next page. B and C speak English. Put an X in rows B and C in the English column. D doesn't speak English. Put an O in the D row in the English column.

	Eng.	Sp.	Fr.	Port.	Ital.
A					
B	X				
C	X				
D	O				
E					

50. MISTER DIGIT FACE. Where can 9 go?

51. DIGIT TREE. With the nine digits we have to make 7 numbers. Two numbers will have two digits each. What is the highest number that could be at the top of the tree?

52. FIGURES TO CUT IN TWO. Try several times. There is no definite way. It's a matter of eyesight.

53. SEGMENTS. The sum of all nine digits is 45.

54. MULTIPLE TOWERS. Certain levels must have even numbers.

55. EARTHLINGS. The second earthling had one answer in common with the first one and one in common with the third. Is this earthling honest, a liar, or both?

56. THE ANT AND THE CLOCK. Draw a clock. Draw the path of the ant. Compare distances.

57-59. HIDDEN WORD. Compare the words in column 0 with the others. If one letter appears in the same position in column 0 and also in another, you can cross it out in that column, since you know it will not be in the word in the rectangle.

60-64. SECRET NUMBER. When you know that a digit is not in the secret number, cross it out. If you discover that a digit is in the secret number, but don't know where, circle it. When you find its correct position, mark it with a square. Do this for all lines. Make a list of the digits that are definitely in the secret number, another for those that are not in the secret number, and a third list for those you are not sure about.

65-70. DOMINOES. Cross out the dominoes that are already placed in the list. Let's imagine that the domino

3-4 has already been placed. Separate every other instance of 3 and 4 together in the table (remember, dominoes only appear once). Then look for pairs of numbers that are together (like 5 and 6, for example) and do the same. As you go from one puzzle to the next, you will think of more strategies.

71. HOUND—I. If you think of the distances between the marked squares you can place the number 10. Think of where the odd and even numbers go.

72. HOUND—II. The lower left box is 21.

73. HOUND—III. The lower left box is 25.

74. HOUND—IV. The lower left box is 1.

75. HOUND—V. We have 9 prime numbers. To obtain a symmetric figure, we must have the same quantity of prime numbers on the left as on the right.

If we paint the board like a checkerboard with a black diagonal, we will have 12 white squares and 13 black ones. Where do the prime numbers go?

76-81. POKER. The straight combinations are the most useful information for you at first, especially the straight flushes. Four of a kind is also useful. Remember that all straights must have a 10 and a J, and that a four of a kind has four cards of equal value. If for a certain card you have two possible values, consider each value individually until you find the solution.

Answers

1. Twins

I spoke to Peter. If a person always lies or alternately, always tells the truth, he cannot admit that he is lying (if this person were a liar, he would be telling the truth, and if this person were honest, he would be lying). Therefore, Paul could not have answered my question. Peter could answer about Paul without contradicting himself. What we don't know is who the liar is.

2. Twin Statistics

More than 3% of the population are twins. Out of 100 births, 97 are single and 3 are twins. That's 103 babies in total, six of which are twins, which represents 5.8% of the population.

3. Place Your Cards

From left to right: queen of spades, six of diamonds, and ace of hearts.

4. The Professor and His Friend

Professor Zizoloziz wins. Every player takes an odd number of matches per play. After the first player goes, there will always be an odd number of matches left. After the second player goes, there will always be an even number of matches left. Therefore, the second player is the winner.

5. Irregular Circuit

300 yards from point A. The first passing point can be considered as a new starting point. Therefore, the new passing point will be 150 yards away.

6. Economical Progression

1, 6, 11, 16, 21, 26. Other solutions are also possible.

7. Skin and Shoes
It is enough to look at only one shoe. If, for example, the white man's right shoe is red, the left one has to be black. This means that the black man will have one left red shoe and one right white shoe, and so on.

8. Up and Down
22 steps. While Zizoloziz goes up the entire staircase, I descend the staircase except for 11 steps (7 at the top + 4 at the bottom). Since he goes twice as fast as me, the entire staircase is 2 × 11 steps.

9. What Month—I
February of a leap year. If a month starts and ends with the same day of the week, it must have a complete number of weeks plus one more day. The only possible month is a 29-day February.

10. What Month—II
August. In order to add up to 38, it can only be the highest possible number for the last Monday of a month (31) and the highest for the first Thursday of a month (7). Therefore, both last month and the current must have 31 days. The only two 31-day months in a row in the same calendar year are July and August.

11. Eve's Enigma
Thursday. The snake is lying, because it says that today is Saturday and tomorrow is Wednesday. Therefore, today is one of the days when the snake lies (Tuesday, Thursday, and Saturday). It cannot be Saturday or else the snake would not be lying in one statement. Nor can it be Tuesday, for the same reason. It can only be Thursday.

12. Broken M

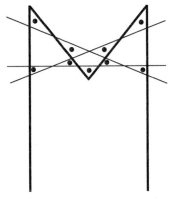

13. Soccer Scores—I

The Eagles had 5 points. There were 10 matches in the tournament with a total of 20 points to be won by the teams. The table already has 15 points assigned. Therefore, the remaining 5 points must belong to the Eagles.

14. Soccer Scores—II

Lions 0, Tigers 0. Lions 1, Bears 0. Tigers 1, Bears 1. The Lions could only win 3 points by wining one match and tying another. Since they only scored one goal, the results must be 1-0 and 0-0. The Bears tied one and lost the other match. The scores must have been 1-1 and 0-1. Their tied game must have been against the Tigers. So the Lions beat the Bears 1-0, and the Lions tied the Tigers 0-0.

15. What Time Is It—I

5:00. From here, the minute hand will take 30 minutes to reach 6, and the hour hand will take an entire hour.

16. What Time Is It—II

There are two possible times in this situation: 5:15 (the minute hand takes 15 minutes to reach 6 and the hour hand takes 45) and 3:45 (the minute hand takes 45 minutes to reach 6 and the hour hand takes 2 hours and 15 minutes, which is 135 minutes).

17. What Time Is It—III

2:12. The hour hand is at the first minute mark after 2, and the minute hand is on the next minute mark.

18. What Time Is It—IV

9:48. The minute hand is on 48 minutes and the hour hand is on the next minute mark.

19. Prohibited Connection

Each middle digit (2, 3, 4, and 5) can only be connected to three others (for example, 2 can only be connected to 4, 5, and 6). There are two circles with four connections. We can only put 1 and 6 in them. Once you insert these, the rest is easy to figure out. Another solution exists where the order of the numbers is switched, so 1 and 6 switch, as do 2 and 5, and 3 and 4.

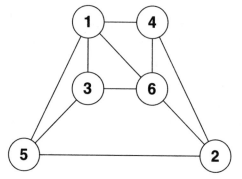

20. Concentric

30 square inches. We turn the small square as shown in the picture on the next page. We can see that it is half the size of the big one, as indicated by the dotted lines. These dotted lines divide the large square into 8 triangles, and the small square into 4 triangles.

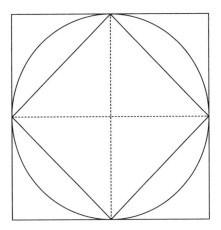

21. John Cash

The reward was 125 dollars. If you erase 1, you have 25 left, which is one fifth the original amount. If you erase 2, you have 5 left, which is one fifth of this amount.

To get 125, find a two-digit number in which you can take the first digit off and the result is one fifth of the number. The only possible number is 25. 25 × 5 = 125.

22. Russian Roulette

The arsenic is in the jar labeled "SUGAR." We know that the snuff is above the salt. They cannot be on the right side, because then the salt would be in the jar labeled "SALT." They cannot be in the center either, because then the second answer would not be true since the coffee and sugar would not be next to each other. Therefore, they are on the left. So the coffee and sugar are in the jars marked "TEA" and "SALT," respectively, leaving arsenic for either the jar marked "ARSENIC" or "SUGAR." Since it's not in the correctly labeled jar, it must be in the jar marked "SUGAR," and the tea is in the jar marked "ARSENIC."

23. New Race

One car goes twice as fast as the other. The first crossing took place at point A. Consider A as a new starting point. Do the same for every crossing point. Since they drove at consistent speeds, the distances from A to B, B to C, and C to A are the same. After point A, one car must have driven twice the distance as the other to reach B at the same time. Therefore, one goes twice as fast as the other.

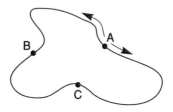

24. The Calculator Keys

There are two possibilities:
   1. Change the 4 with the 5 and the 2 with the 8.
   $729 - 546 = 183$.
   2. Change the 3 with the 9 and the 4 with the 6.
   $783 - 654 = 129$.

25. Nice Discounts

You first buy books for $80 and, the next day, for $70, which represents a discount of $70 × .08 = $5.60. (It will be the same result by inverting the order of the purchases, first the $70 purchase and the next day the $80 one.)

26. Enigmatic Fares

98999 and 99000. The tickets are consecutive in number. If the professor had answered "yes" to the question about the five digits of one ticket adding up to 35, the friend could have not figured out the numbers. There would have been several possibilities (78659 and 78660, 36989 and 36990, etc.), so the professor must have answered that indeed none of the tickets added up to 35.

   Both tickets add up to 62 (an even number), which

means that the first one must end in a 9. If it ended in only one 9, one ticket would add up to 35. Let's call the first ticket ABCD9 and the second one ABC(D + 1)0. The sum is A + B + C + D + 9 + A + B + C + D + 1 = 62, meaning that A + B + C + D + 9 = 35. If it ended in two 9s, the sum of both tickets would give us an odd number.

Therefore, the ticket must end in three 9s and no more than three, or the sum wouldn't be 62. We can call the tickets AB999 and A(B+1)000, where B is not 9. The sum of both is $2 \times (A + B) + 28 = 62$. Therefore, A = 9 and B = 8.

27. Horoscope

The teacher is a Pisces. This conversation could have only taken place on February 29. She was 29 then. Six days later (March 6), having turned 30, it becomes true that the date is one fifth of her age. This means her birthday occurs during the six first days of March.

28. Strangers in the Night

The blonde woman killed Mr. Farnanski. There are only four true statements. Only one person is guilty. Therefore, three of the "I'm innocent" statements are true. Only one more statement can be true, and this must be the one made by the man in the dark suit or by the blonde woman. Therefore, "The brunette killed him" and "One of the men killed him" are false statements, so the blonde woman is the killer.

29. Monte Carlo

He lost. Every time that Hystrix wins, his money increases 1.5 times (with $100, he bets $50 and if he wins, he has $150). When he loses, his money is reduced by half. So a win-loss combination results in a loss of one quarter of his money. The more he plays, the more money he loses, even though he wins the same number of times as he loses.

30. The Foreigners and the Menu
They could have ordered ABCDD their first night (finding out what D is), AEFGG the second night (finding out what G is and what A is, since they had ordered it the previous night, too), and BEHII the third night, (finding out what I, B, and E are). This leaves C, F, and H out, and since they had never ordered these dishes twice and each came on a different night, they should know what they are.

31. Fort Knox Jumping Frogs—I
Move 5 onto 2, 3 onto 7, 1 onto 4, and 6 onto 8.

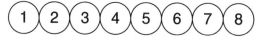

32. Fort Knox Jumping Frogs—II
Move 5 onto 2, 3 onto 7, 4 onto 13, 6 onto 1, 12 onto 9, 11 onto 14, and 10 onto 8.

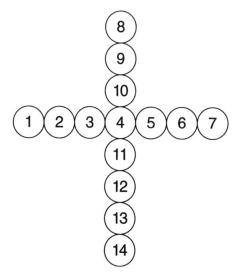

33. Fort Knox Jumping Frogs—III

Move 5 onto 12, 6 onto 4, 10 onto 11, 8 onto 1, 3 onto 2, and 9 onto 7.

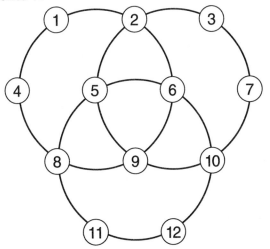

34. Fort Knox Jumping Frogs—IV

Move 16 onto 3, 8 onto 5, 17 onto 11, 10 onto 18, 2 onto 15, 7 onto 1, 13 onto 9, 14 onto 20, 12 onto 19, and 6 onto 4.

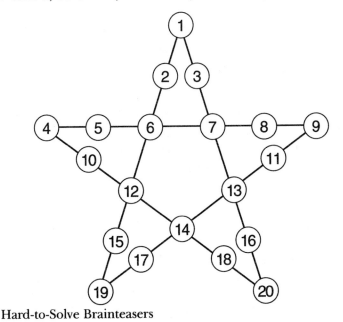

35. Fort Knox Jumping Frogs—V
Move 1 onto 4, 10 onto 7, 11 onto 14, 20 onto 17, 5 onto 3, 6 onto 8, 15 onto 13, 16 onto 18, 2 onto 12, and 19 onto 9.

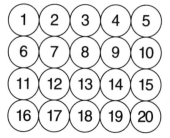

36. The Harem
There were seven locks. Let's name the locks A, B, C, D, E, F, and G. The vizier had keys for A, B, C, D, E, and F. One of the slaves had the keys for A, B, C, and G. Another one, for A, D, E, and G. Another, for B, D, F, and G. And the last, for C, E, F, and G. With seven locks, the Great Tamerlan's system works—but not with fewer locks.

37. The Dividing End
The number is 381654729.

If the number is ABCDEFGHI, B, D, F, and H are even numbers. The rest are odd numbers. ABCDE can be divided evenly by 5, thus E = 5.

ABCD can be divided evenly by 4. Therefore, CD can also be divided evenly by 4, and since C is an odd number, D can only be 2 or 6.

ABCDEF can be divided evenly by 6 (by 2 and by 3). Since ABC can be divided by 3, DEF can be also. Consequently, DEF is 258 or 654.

You can deduce the rest from here.

38. The Island and the Englishmen

Six Englishmen. Let's draw four circles representing the clubs. Every two clubs have one member in common, so we draw a line from each circle to one point (an Englishman). Each dot is connected to two lines. This is the situation in the illustration, indicating six Englishmen.

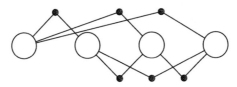

39. Logic Apples

Alonso 1, Bertrand 2, George 3, and Kurt 5.

Alonso could not have eaten 5 or more. Bertrand could not have eaten only one or he would have known that he hadn't eaten more than Alonso. Neither could he have eaten 5 or more. He could have eaten 2, 3, or 4. George figures this out, although he still doesn't know if he ate more than Bertrand. This means that George must have eaten 3 or 4. Kurt can only deduce the other amounts if he ate 5. And the rest, in order to add up to 11, must have eaten 1, 2, and 3.

40. Added Corners

The 8 cannot be in a corner, so we have to put it in a square. The 7 must go in a square too. This makes it easy to figure out the rest.

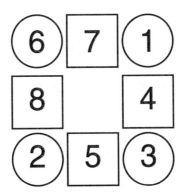

41. Rectangles

Both rectangles have the same area, 40 square inches. If you draw the dotted line you will see that the line divides the inclined figure into two equal pairs of triangles on both sides.

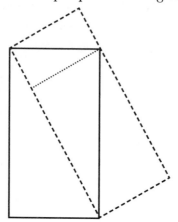

42. A Warm Farewell

10 men and 6 women. The number of handshakes and kisses adds up to 55. Each Porter said good-bye to each Robinson. If we multiply the number of members of both families, the result should be 55. There are two possibilities: $55 = 11 \times 5$ (one family with 11 members and other one with 5), or $55 = 55 \times 1$ (which could not be possible, since a family is not formed by only one person).

We now analyze the handshakes following the same procedure. There are two possibilities: $21 = 7 \times 3$ (7 men in one family and 3 in the other) or $21 = 21 \times 1$ (which could not be possible, because none of these families has so many members, as seen above). Therefore, one family is formed by 7 men and 4 women, and the other by 3 men and 2 women.

43. Four Minus One Is a Crime

The killer is Mr. A. To go from A to B you will always travel an even number of blocks. However, in the statements there is an odd number (13 blocks from A to the corner of the meeting and from there to B's house). So, either A or B is lying. A similar condition applies to A and C. You will need an odd number of blocks, but the statements talk about an even number. So, either A or C is lying. Therefore, A is lying.

44. On the Route of Marco Polo

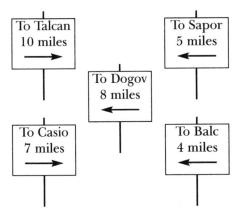

The road signs each point to a different village. The sum of distances in one direction and the sum in the opposite direction must be equal. This can only be achieved with 10 + 7 = 8 + 5 + 4. Therefore, the signs with 10 and 7 point in one direction and the three others point in the opposite direction.

45. On the Road
10 miles from Philadelphia.

The five signs indicate the following distances: 98, 76, 54, 32, 10.

Other possible sequences include: 90, 81, 72, 63, 54 and 90, 72, 54, 36, 18. However, in all cases the distance from the final sign to Philadelphia is greater.

46. Touching Squares

14 squares.

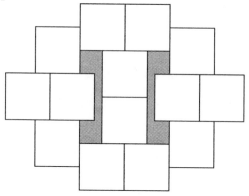

47. Equal Vision

Six watchmen. One way to do it is shown below.

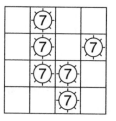

48. Blood and Sand

Lincoln Dustin died at 5:30. At first the commissioner thought that Mr. Dustin had inverted the hourglass at 7:30 (which would account for the 15 hours that the hourglass took to finish). The evident suspect is Begonias, who was at the mansion at the time. Then Begonias told him that he had inverted the hourglass. This made the commissioner think that Mr. Dustin had inverted the hourglass and then Begonias did as well, which means that the time between both inversions counted twice toward the total amount of time. Since the total time was 3 hours, Begonias inverted the hourglass one and a half hours after Mr. Dustin had. If Begonias said that he had inverted it at 7 P.M., this means that Mr. Dustin inverted it at 5:30.

Hard-to-Solve Brainteasers

49. International Summit

A-Spanish, French, Portuguese; B-all; C-all except French; D-Spanish; and E-French and Italian.

Draw a table with five rows and five columns, making the languages the column headers and the people the row headers. Statement 1 tells us that B and C speak English. Mark an X in the corresponding cells. Statement 1 also tells us that D does not speak English. Mark a zero in the corresponding cell. Additionally, statement 1 tells us B, C, and D speak Spanish. Mark it in the table. Follow the same procedure for statement 2 and statement 3. Statement 3 explains that the only common language to C and E is Italian, and since C also speaks English and Spanish, we can write zeroes for E in those columns. In a similar way, write a zero for French in C.

This is how the table will look at this point:

	Eng.	Sp.	Fr.	Port.	Ital.
A			X		
B	X	X	X		
C	X	X	O		X
D	O	X			
E	O	O	X		X

We can see that three people speak Spanish and French. Add another X for Spanish, since it is the most common language.

From statement 6 we need one person who speaks only one language. The only possibility is D. Complete the row with zeroes. From statement 4 we look for the three people who speak Portuguese. They cannot be C and E, since their common language was Italian. Therefore, two of the Portuguese speakers must be A and B. From statement 6 we need a person who speaks only two languages. It can only be E, so we write a zero for E in Portuguese. The third person who speaks Portuguese must be C, so we mark an X in the corresponding cell. We look now for the person who speaks three languages, and it can only be A. Fill in the row with zeroes. So, the person who speaks five languages is B. The table is now complete.

50. Mister Digit Face

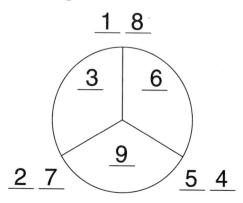

The 9 must be inside the circle, because no product can be 9_ or _9. The 1, 2, and 5 must be outside the circle. From here on you can find the solution. (Other answers can be made by flipping or rotating the circle.)

51. Digit Tree

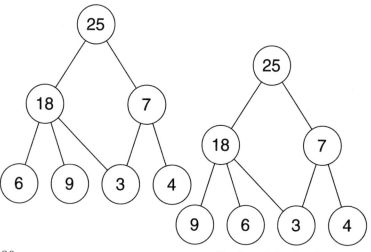

52. Figures to Cut in Two

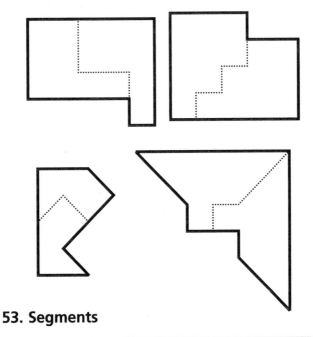

53. Segments

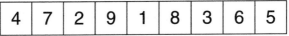

The numbers 4 and 5 must be at both ends because the sum of the nine digits is 45. Then we place 3 and 6, then 2 and 7, and finally 1, 8, and 9. (The order of the numbers can be reversed.)

54. Multiple Towers

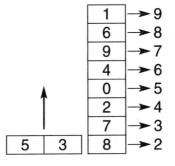

55. Earthlings

Uruguay came in first, Spain second, Zaire third. The second earthling has one answer in common with the first one and one in common with the third one. In which category is the second earthling, then? He cannot always be telling the truth, because he has something in common with a liar, and he cannot always be lying because he has something in common with the honest one. If his first answer were true, then the third one would also be true, and they would be the same as the first and third answers from the honest man. There is no match, however, so this is not the case.

Therefore, the first answer from the man that alternately lies and tells the truth must be a lie. The second is true and the third a lie, so the third man is the honest one, and thus the his answers are the results of the soccer championship.

56. The Ant and the Clock

The ant walked 54 minutes. From the first meeting to the second, the minute hand traveled 45 minutes and the ant a distance in minute marks of 105 minutes (45 + a complete 60-minute lap). The illustration below shows the path followed by the ant. The speed ratio is 45/105 = 3/7. From the start to the first meeting, the minute hand traveled a distance X and the ant (30 − X). Using the speed ratio, this would be X/(30 − X) = 3/7. X = 9 minutes. If we add these to the 45 minutes that it took the ant to get to the second meeting, we come to 54 minutes for the ant's trip.

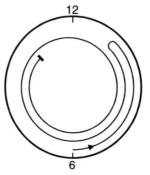

Hard-to-Solve Brainteasers

57. Hidden Word—I
VISE

58. Hidden Word—II
SOB

59. Hidden Word—III
PITHY

60. Secret Number—I
3719

61. Secret Number—II
9381

62. Secret Number—III
2754

63. Secret Number—IV
2739

64. Secret Number—V
8327

65. Dominoes Table I

1	5	5	3	0	6	0	6
5	4	4	2	4	4	6	2
2	6	0	1	1	2	5	1
4	3	5	5	3	2	6	0
0	3	0	3	3	3	1	0
5	2	6	2	3	6	0	1
4	5	6	4	1	4	2	1

66. Dominoes Table II

3	1	2	2	6	1	3	4
5	5	3	4	0	5	3	2
2	6	5	1	1	2	0	0
1	1	0	6	0	3	3	0
0	6	4	3	6	5	4	5
3	2	5	4	0	1	6	2
5	4	6	4	2	4	6	1

Hard-to-Solve Brainteasers

67. Dominoes Table III

1	0	2	2	3	6	5
1	6	6	4	3	6	5
2	3	5	0	1	4	6
0	4	3	0	2	4	0
3	6	5	4	5	4	1
0	0	5	1	3	1	2
3	6	2	2	5	3	2
1	1	4	0	4	6	5

68. Dominoes Table IV

5	4	2	3	6	3	4
4	6	5	5	0	6	3
4	6	2	3	4	1	2
6	0	6	3	0	4	1
0	6	0	2	3	4	2
5	5	6	1	4	5	3
5	1	3	2	2	1	1
1	5	2	0	1	0	0

69. Dominoes Table V

4	0	0	1	1	1	0
5	2	3	5	6	5	6
3	5	4	4	3	4	2
2	0	0	5	6	5	3
2	2	1	5	6	0	1
2	4	4	3	2	6	4
5	6	0	3	2	3	6
1	1	3	6	4	1	0

70. Dominoes Table VI

4	5	1	6	0	5	1
2	5	3	5	3	6	5
6	2	0	4	2	2	6
6	6	2	0	5	3	3
3	1	1	2	3	6	4
4	0	3	1	0	0	4
4	1	2	1	4	5	3
5	1	2	0	0	4	6

71. Hound—I

20	13	12	11	(10)
19	14	(5)	6	9
18	(15)	4	7	8
17	16	3	2	1

72. Hound—II

25	26	27	(28)	29	30	31
24	15	(14)	(35)	34	33	32
23	16	13	12	11	8	(7)
22	17	18	1	10	9	6
(21)	20	19	2	3	4	5

73. Hound—III

2	1	9	10	11
3	8	16	15	12
4	7	17	14	13
5	6	18	19	20
25	24	23	22	21

74. Hound—IV

25	16	15	12	11
24	17	14	13	10
23	22	21	20	9
2	3	18	19	8
1	4	5	6	7

75. Hound—V

There are two possible solutions.

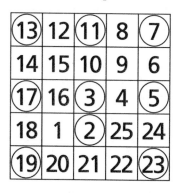

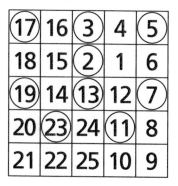

76. Poker—I

J	10	J	K	A
8	8	8	A	8
Q	10	A	Q	Q
K	10	K	10	K
A	9	9	9	9

77. Poker—II

9	J	10	Q	K
J	J	Q	Q	Q
A	A	A	A	K
8	J	10	8	K
10	9	10	8	K

78.Poker—III

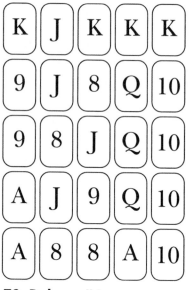

K	J	K	K	K
9	J	8	Q	10
9	8	J	Q	10
A	J	9	Q	10
A	8	8	A	10

79. Poker—IV

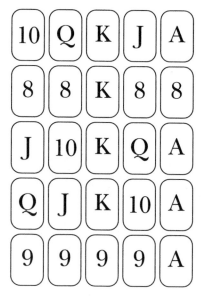

10	Q	K	J	A
8	8	K	8	8
J	10	K	Q	A
Q	J	K	10	A
9	9	9	9	A

Hard-to-Solve Brainteasers

80. Poker—V

9	A	9	A	A
8	Q	K	K	10
8	Q	K	J	J
8	A	9	J	10
8	Q	9	J	10

81. Poker—VI

10	Q	Q	Q	10
9	K	J	Q	10
A	K	A	A	A
8	K	J	8	10
J	K	J	8	9

Index

Key: puzzle, *hint*, **answer**

Added Corners, 25, *61*, **75**
Ant and the Clock, The, 35, *62*, **82**
Blood and Sand, 30-31, *61*, **78**
Broken M, 10, *59*, **67**
Calculator Keys, The, 15, *60*, **70**
Concentric, 13, *60*, **68-69**
Digit Tree, 32, *62*, **80**
Dividing End, The, 24, *61*, **74**
Dominoes, 41-47, *62-63*, **84-86**
Earthlings, 35, *62*, **82**
Economical Progression, 8, *59*, **65**
Enigmatic Fares, 16, *60*, **70-71**
Equal Vision, 29, *61*, **78**
Eve's Enigma, 9, *59*, **66**
Figures to Cut in Two, 33, *62*, **81**
Foreigners and the Menu, The, 18, *60*, **72**
Fort Knox Jumping Frogs, 19-23, *60*, **72-74**
Four Minus One Is a Crime, 27, *61*, **76-77**
Harem, The, 24, *60*, **74**
Hidden Word, 36-37, *62*, **83**
Horoscope, 16, *60*, **71**
Hound, 48-50, *63*, **87-88**
International Summit, 31, *61-62*, **79-80**
Irregular Circuit, 7, *59*, **65**
Island and the Englishmen, The, 24, *61*, **75**
John Cash, 13, *60*, **69**
Logic Apples, 25, *61*, **75**
Mister Digit Face, 32, *62*, **80**
Monte Carlo, 18, *60*, **71**
Multiple Towers, 34, *62*, **81**
New Race, 15, *60*, **70**
Nice Discounts, 16, *60*, **70**
On the Road, 28, *61*, **77**
On the Route of Marco Polo, 28, *61*, **77**

Place Your Cards, 6, *59*, **65**
Poker, 51-57, *63*, **89-91**
Professor and His Friend, The, 7, *59*, **65**
Prohibited Connection, 12, *60*, **68**
Rectangles, 26, *61*, **76**
Russian Roulette, 14, *60*, **69**
Secret Number, 38-40, *62*, **83**
Segments, 34, *62*, 81
Skin and Shoes, 8, *59*, **66**
Soccer Scores, 11, *59*, **67**
Strangers in the Night, 17, *60*, **71**
Touching Squares, 29, *61*, **78**
Twins, 6, *59*, **65**
Twin Statistics, 6, *59*, **65**
Up and Down, 8, *59*, **66**
Warm Farewell, A, 26, *61*, **76**
What Month, 9, *59*, **66**
What Time Is It, 11-12, *60*, **67-68**

What Is American Mensa?

American Mensa
The High IQ Society

One out of 50 people qualifies
for American Mensa ...
Are YOU the One?

American Mensa, Ltd. is an organization for individuals who have one common trait: a score in the top two percent of the population on a standardized intelligence test. Over five million Americans are eligible for membership ... you may be one of them.

• Looking for intellectual stimulation?
You'll find a good "mental workout" in the *Mensa Bulletin*, our national magazine. Voice your opinion in the newsletter published by your local group. And attend activities and gatherings with fascinating programs and engaging conversation.

• Looking for social interaction?
There's something happening on the Mensa calendar almost daily. These range from lectures to game nights to parties. Each year, there are over 40 regional gatherings and the Annual Gathering, where you can meet people, exchange ideas, and make interesting new friends.

• Looking for others who share your special interest?
Whether your interest might be as common as computer gaming or as esoteric as eugenics, there's probably a Mensa Special Interest Group (SIG) for you. There are over 150 SIGs, which are started and maintained by members.

So contact us today to receive a free brochure and application.

American Mensa, Ltd.
1229 Corporate Drive West
Arlington, TX 76006
(800) 66-MENSA
AmericanMensa@compuserve.com
http://www.us.mensa.org

If you don't live in the U.S. and would like to get in touch with your national Mensa, contact:

Mensa International
15 The Ivories
6-8 Northampton Street, Islington
London N1 2HY England

About the Authors

JAIME PONIACHIK was born in Uruguay and resides in neighboring Argentina, where he is well-known as a creator of games and mathematical recreations. He has been a long-time puzzle columnist in magazines, and also gives lectures on the subject. He is the publisher of Ediciones De Mente, which puts out crossword puzzle magazines, books, and board games. He enjoys reading, playing ping pong, and walking on the beach or in the mountains.

LEA PONIACHIK née Gorodisky was born in Argentina and has a degree in mathematics. She was a member of the Argentine team that came in second place at the 1992 World Puzzle Championship held in New York City.

Jaime and Lea live in Buenos Aires with their son John, their daughter Nina, their cat Gris, and their dog Caissa.